Meditation

Stress Relief is a Breath Away

By

E. J. Finizio, M.A.

For sale on

Amazon.com

This book is dedicated to my parents

Victor and Ruth Finizio,

who supported me when no one else did.

I hope that this book is something you can be proud of.

Thank you for everything.

Meditation: Stress relief is a breath away

Introduction

This book is a collection of different types of meditations, with each exercise preceded with a short description of it's purpose and use.

Believe it or not, there are many different types of meditations, more than even this book holds. Each type has a different ultimate goal in mind – spiritual insight, easing recuperation from surgery, preventing relapses, and so on – yet there is one lesser goal that meditations all have in common. They slow down the resting heart rate through non-chemical, totally holistic and natural means, thus reducing the level of stress in the individual meditating.

An excess of stress is very unhealthy if experienced on a regular basis, and can manifest in symptoms ranging from emotional discomfort to physical pain or disease. Through meditation, a person can

3

take back control of their physical, emotional, and psychological functioning, and they can do it without introducing artificial substances into their systems. Similarly, meditation is often used to augment anti-anxiety and other medications aimed at reducing the resting heart rate in the patient, or in place of such medications but still in conjunction with others as part of recuperation or other medical regiment.

So, what have you got to lose? Read a chapter here and there when you find you have time & become curious, try the meditation at the end, and enjoy better health. Even if you find that meditation is not for you (though I find that it often takes a few attempts to stick, but, once stuck, people miss their daily meditation time when they don't experience it) wasn't this something new to try, if only to say "yeah, I tried that." With no adverse side effects possible (unlike popular medication regimens) what have you got to lose?

Table of Contents

Chapter 9: "**Disciplined Moving**"
meditation to music *[Advanced]*

Endnote

*Blank pages to use to begin a meditation
journal are included at the end of this book.*

Chapter 1: Intro To Breathing

As I mentioned in the introduction, most of us are not breathing properly. We don't know the difference between diaphragm breathing and shallow breathing, we don't pay much attention to whether we breathe through our nose or our mouth, and we certainly don't pay attention to how long it takes for us to inhale or exhale, or how long we hold air in or out between breaths.

Not here.

The very first and most important part of any meditation exercise is to learn how be mindful of your breathing, and then to apply that knowledge by breathing more deeply.

There is a very simple way to become aware of whether we are breathing deeply or shallowly, and this test can be performed anywhere, and without anyone around us knowing that we are doing it:

Place your hand on your stomach and inhale.

(That's it. That's the entire exercise.)

Did your hand move?

If it did, you are breathing through your diaphragm, which is the right way to breathe. Good for you!

Now, let's try to ensure that those breaths get deeper, can be held longer, and are not the result of "combination breathing" which is when both our diaphragms and shoulders move, and which is not as good as proper diaphragm breathing.

If your hand did not move, chances are your shoulders did. When we breathe into our chest cavity only, and not our diaphragms, our shoulders move up to accommodate the expansion of our chest cavity due to the influx of air. This is called "shallow breathing," and it does not ensure that enough oxygen is reaching our lungs for proper respiratory health.

It is helpful to note that diaphragm breathing and the relaxation that occurs as a result of meditation will work in conjunction with each other. That is, the better one gets at diaphragm breathing, the easier it is to induce deep relaxation through meditation. Also, the better one gets at meditating, the easier it will be to induce diaphragm breathing. The Tense and Release chapter especially can help when one is first learning how to breathe properly.

The key here is to "allow" rather than "cause" the diaphragm breathing.

"What happens to my breath if I give up control totally?" your body will keep breathing to keep you alive.

What does that feel like? It's nature at work, not you in control. Co-operate with nature.

Babies breathe diaphragmatically from birth, and only stop doing so when something gets in the way.

The trick is to get out of your own way, to be aware of what is happening when the breathing is out of conscious control.

Inducing Diaphragm Breathing:

Lie on your back on the floor and place your hand over your stomach.

Let every aspect of your body soften totally.

After a minute lazily flop a hand on your belly and pay attention to what's happening.

The important thing is to give up control of any kind. The diaphragm breathing will be automatic.

Once you've been able to feel it happening automatically, you can sit in a chair, and, finally, stand up and remember the feeling, and permit it to happen again. It can all be done in a sequence.

Measured Breath:

Many people have a hard time simply releasing control of their breathing.

So, as a preliminary step to naturally occurring diaphragmatic breathing, there is a technique called Measured Breath, in which one inhales through the nose and exhales through the mouth, counting the spaces between breaths and the seconds the inhale and exhale takes.

The idea is to cause longer, deeper breaths through practice, and to observe this by counting higher.

Measured Breath:

Inhale through your nose.

Pause

Exhale through your mouth.

Pause.

Again.

Pause.

This time, as you inhale through your nose, try to count slowly to 4 before stopping.

Pause

Good.

Now, as you exhale through your mouth, count slowly to 4 before stopping.

Pause.

Good!

This time, count to 4 on the inhale through your nose,

hold for a count of four,

and exhale naturally through your mouth.

Pause

Excellent.

Finally, inhale through your nose for a count of four,

hold for a count of four,

exhale through your mouth for a count of four,

and hold your breath out for a count of four.

Then repeat the process.

Pause.

Very good!

Measured Breath should be practiced whenever possible in order to master the technique. As you continue to practice, try holding each part of the breath longer by counting higher.

The longer the breath, the deeper the breath, and the more oxygen you will be getting into your lungs.

Chapter 2: Safe Place Meditation

Safe Place meditations are used in the field of psychology as part of holistic wellness regimens, predominantly with chemical and behavior addicts (such as alcoholics, compulsive gamblers, over eaters and so on) and also with clients who show signs of PTSD (people who have survived traumatic situations and no longer feel safe because of it).

During my second-year Master's internship at the Brien Center in Massachusetts, I used Safe Place meditations with dual diagnosis (meaning they were diagnosed with a chemical dependency, such as opiate addiction, and also with a mental health disorder) in both one-on-one and group sessions, and I saw a remarkable reduction of symptoms in the clients who fully participated and took the meditations seriously.

This is not a research-based psychology book with mathematical statistics run on data to find significant correlations for meditation. I'm just reporting anecdotally that I saw a difference in a clinical setting.

Now, I list my Safe Place meditation as a "beginner" level of guided meditation. This is absolutely true if you are listening to a guide who is telling you what to do as the meditation progresses.

I'm currently working on a Safe Place Meditation CD so that readers can have this experience that my private clients receive, even if they live far away or otherwise can't book a session.

However, to actually do this meditation from print in a book is very difficult, as it is a fully guided meditation and is not intended to be interrupted by reading. Also, this particular meditation is best performed by someone who has been trained in guiding meditations because there are certain word and tone emphases that must be incorporated for the effect to be optimal.

The one that I wrote for use with clients at the Brien Center is the one I'm including in this book. My suggestion is that you read it just to see what it is, and if you're interested in trying it, get the CD when it comes out. Or, you can ask a friend to read the meditation out of the book to you, and try it that way. It's up to you.

Safe Place meditations are intended to be repeated once a day every day. They take 15-35 minutes depending on the client and how many times he or she has made this journey before. I usually allow more time during each of the pauses for clients who have already made the journey many times before.

When clients are new they often ask how long the meditation took, and when I answer about 15 minutes, they exclaim: "That long? It felt like less than five minutes!"

Safe Place Meditation:

This is a safe place meditation. We are going to take a journey today.

Get into a comfortable position on the floor or in a chair, sit back, and relax.

Allow your eyes to close or to rest on some object in the room.

Feel your mind wander. Let all your thoughts amble around, and pass by.

As I count down from 10, I want you to let yourself become more and more relaxed, and fall deeper and deeper asleep, breathing in through your nose, and out through your mouth.

10 – feel your body become heavy

9 – breathe in through your nose, and out through your mouth

8 - breathe in, hold, breath out

7 – feel your mind continue to wander

6 – in, out

4 – you begin to see the outline of a place

3 – this place comes more clearly into focus

2 - you can touch the land and smell the smells now

1 - you are there

You are completely in your safe place. You can see things clearly, smell what there is to smell, touch what there is to touch.

What does this place look like? What does it feel like? What does it smell like?

Take a moment to experience this place.

Pause

What does this place look like?

Pause

What does it feel like to be here?

Pause

What smells and sounds are there to experience in this place?

Pause

It's wonderful here, isn't it?

Pause

This place is a very special place. This is your Safe Place, and you can always come back to it, no matter what.

Once you leave, you can always return.

Pause

All you need to do to return, is to close your eyes, imagine being here, and breathe.

Pause

We are going to begin our return journey now. As I count up from 1 to 10, you will gradually begin to come back.

1 – look around; you can always come back

2- detach from what you're doing

3- see the place fade; outlines become fuzzy

4- remember to breathe in through the nose, and out through the mouth

5 – breathe in, out

6- feel how comfortable your body feels in this position

7 - wiggle your toes

8- stretch your muscles; you've been here a long time

9- yawn

10-open your eyes!

You are now back in the room

Pause

Welcome back

Allow time for people to make the transition back, while tethering them to the physical room by turning off the background music and beginning the post-meditation conversational debriefing.

Chapter 3: Tense and Release Body Meditation

Not all meditation takes place entirely in the mind. In fact, I find that one of the easiest types of meditation for beginners to work with is a type of body-focus meditation called Tense and Release. As the name suggests, this type of meditation involves tensing up different body parts (for example, "make a fist and squeeze it tight" is one of the instructions) then holding that tension, breathing, and releasing the tension as you release the breath.

Tense and Release meditation is excellent for physical ailments and discomforts that are caused or exacerbated by muscle tension. They are also an excellent type of meditation for beginners, because we tend to be a body-oriented society, and the tactile element of focusing on your body one muscle at a time helps to build a state of mindfulness that can be transferred over to other types of meditation.

Tense and Release Body Meditation:

Sit in a chair in a comfortable position.

Be sure that you're sitting comfortably but with good posture, both feet on the floor, arms resting on armrests or your lap.

We are going to go through this muscle by muscle, so the exercise will require some patience and some focus.

When you are ready to begin, keep reading.

First, tighten your right and into a fist and clench it tight. If you have a tennis ball or a stress ball, feel free to clench it to get your muscles and grip tighter.

Hold it clenched.

I'm going to count out ten seconds, and I need you to keep your muscles clenched until I hit "1".

10-mississippi, 9-mississippi, 8-mississippi, 7-mississippi, 6-mississippi, 5-mississippi, 4-mississippi, 3-mississippi, 2-mississippi, 1

Relax your hand and let it drop open. Let the ball you're holding fall to the floor and let your hand hang limply from your wrist.

Really feel how good this relaxed sensation is. Savor how your right hand feels.

Now, tighten your left hand into a fist and clench it tight. If you have a tennis ball or a stress ball, feel free to clench it to get your muscles and grip tighter.

Hold it clenched.

I'm going to count out ten seconds, and I need you to keep your muscles clenched until I hit "1".

10-mississippi, 9-mississippi, 8-mississippi, 7-mississippi, 6-mississippi, 5-mississippi, 4-mississippi, 3-mississippi, 2-mississippi, 1

Relax your hand and let it drop open. Let the ball you're holding fall to the floor and let your hand hang limply from your wrist.

Shake out your hands; really shake them good before going on to your arms,

Take your right arm and make a muscle. Curl your wrist, brace your elbow and really get your muscles in your arm to clench as tight as they can.

Hold it clenched.

I'm going to count out ten seconds, and I need you to keep your muscles clenched until I hit "1".

10-mississippi, 9-mississippi, 8-mississippi, 7-mississippi, 6-mississippi, 5-mississippi, 4-mississippi, 3-mississippi, 2-mississippi, 1

Relax your arm and shake it out. *Shake-a shake-a shake-a.*

Now, take your left arm and make a muscle. Curl your wrist, brace your elbow and really get your muscles in your arm to clench as tight as they can.

Hold it clenched.

I'm going to count out ten seconds, and I need you to keep your muscles clenched until I hit "1".

10-mississippi, 9-mississippi, 8-mississippi,
7-mississippi, 6-mississippi, 5-mississippi,
4-mississippi, 3-mississippi, 2-mississippi, 1

Relax your arm and shake it out. *Shake-a shake-a shake-a.*

We now move on to the shoulders and neck. Letting the rest of your arm below the shoulder fall limp, scrunch up your shoulders and scrunch down your neck; really try to get your shoulders to touch your ears.

Hold it.

I'm going to count out ten seconds, and I need you to keep your muscles clenched until I hit "1".

10-mississippi, 9-mississippi, 8-mississippi,
7-mississippi, 6-mississippi, 5-mississippi,
4-mississippi, 3-mississippi, 2-mississippi, 1

Relax! Let your shoulders drop down and your head roll. Look to the left, right, down, up, and forward. Stretch out the muscles in your neck.

Now the face. Scrunch up your face as tightly as you can: pucker your lips, clench your jaw, draw in your eyebrows and do anything else you can think of to scrunch-scrunch-scrunch up your face.

I'm going to count out ten seconds, and I need you to keep your muscles clenched until I hit "1".

10-mississippi, 9-mississippi, 8-mississippi, 7-mississippi, 6-mississippi, 5-mississippi, 4-mississippi, 3-mississippi, 2-mississippi, 1

Relax and let your jaw drop! Let your eyelids flutter, stretch out your lips, wiggle eyebrows, and let all that tension that you've been holding in your face go.

Next we move on to the abdomen. Lay flat on the floor, hands locked behind your head with your arms up tight against your ears. Legs should be in sit-up position, bent with feet flat on the floor.

Now, clench your stomach as if you're about to do a sit-up, but only raise your shoulders 6" off the floor.

Hold the position.

I'm going to count out ten seconds, and I need you to keep your muscles clenched until I hit "1".

10-mississippi, 9-mississippi, 8-mississippi, 7-mississippi, 6-mississippi, 5-mississippi, 4-mississippi, 3-mississippi, 2-mississippi, 1

Relax and let everything drop limply to the floor. Lift your arms high over your head and point your toes to stretch out your body before you stand up. Take a moment to relax after stretching; how good does this feel?

Next are the legs. Stand up, and put your right leg on the chair, foot flat on the seat, knee bent at waist height.

Next, angle your left leg slightly by leaning into your right leg until your right leg is pushing your body weight away from the chair, clenched tightly.

Hold that position.

I'm going to count out ten seconds, and I need you to keep your muscles clenched until I hit "1".

10-mississippi, 9-mississippi, 8-mississippi, 7-mississippi, 6-mississippi, 5-mississippi, 4-mississippi, 3-mississippi, 2-mississippi, 1

Relax your right leg by first easing your body weight back onto your left leg, extending your right leg straight, toes pointing up and heel resting comfortably on the chair.

Bend your left leg slightly, and feel the stretch down the back of your right leg.

Next, slowly go back to standing and slowly remove your leg from the chair. Now shake it out hokey-pokey style.

On to the left leg. Standing up, put your left leg on the chair, foot flat on the seat, knee bent at waist height.

Next, angle your right leg slightly by leaning into your left leg until your left leg is pushing your body weight away from the chair, clenched tightly.

Hold that position.

I'm going to count out ten seconds, and I need you to keep your muscles clenched until I hit "1".

10-mississippi, 9-mississippi, 8-mississippi, 7-mississippi, 6-mississippi, 5-mississippi, 4-mississippi, 3-mississippi, 2-mississippi, 1

Relax your left leg by first easing your body weight back onto your right leg, extending your left leg straight, toes pointing up and heel resting comfortably on the chair.

Bend your right leg slightly, and feel the stretch down the back of your left leg.

Next, slowly go back to standing and slowly remove your leg from the chair. Now shake it out hokey-pokey style.

Finally, we come to the feet. Sitting back in the chair, lift your bare feet a few inches off the floor.

Curl your toes and flex your feet so that your leg and foot form a 90 degree angle or tighter.

Hold that position.

I'm going to count out ten seconds, and I need you to keep your muscles clenched until I hit "1".

10-mississippi, 9-mississippi, 8-mississippi, 7-mississippi, 6-mississippi, 5-mississippi, 4-mississippi, 3-mississippi, 2-mississippi, 1

Relax. Shake out your feet, twirl and kick them like you're in a swimming pool; shake them out completely.

Now sit back in your chair and feel your body. Your muscles should feel much less tense than when we started this exercise.

Doesn't it feel good to be relaxed?

Chapter 4: Walk With Nothing Meditation

A Walk With Nothing meditation is very unlike the stereotypical idea of what a meditation is. That is because the mainstream misunderstands the goal of meditation, which is to reduce stress, which allows one to be more aware of the world around them, instead of trapped in the hyper-aroused state of stress that we have gotten used to living with day-to-day.

A Walk With Nothing meditation is a simple relaxation technique that many people have done without necessarily being aware of it. When done deliberately it can be quite an experience. It is intended to help promote mindfulness via experiencing the world more fully through our physical senses.

The "nothing" in Walk With Nothing refers to possessions, including shoes. Leave your purse at home if you have one. Leave behind your wallet, shoes, socks, everything you would normally carry on your person (and everything you would not normally carry, too - no cheating!) keeping with you only the key to your front door, and two articles of clothing to wear: shirt and pants. No shoes or socks, no coat, no underwear – NOTHING!

Now, this may seem like a silly and extreme thing to do. It may seem like it has no real value or purpose. To that assertion, I would like to respond with the following memory: the last time you walked barefoot across wet grass.

Remember it as completely as you can.

Now, how would that memory be different if you had been wearing shoes?

I think my point is proven. Very often, our own experiences in life are our greatest teachers. Re-learning that lesson is a large part of why Walks With Nothing exist.

Walks with Nothing are intended to be performed between once a week to once every few months as needed. They can take place in a variety of locations: urban street blocks, grocery stores, forests, beaches, and so on. While it is a good idea to switch up locations to more fully experience wherever you are, in the beginning walking several times in the same place should bring new observations about that place each time. This is, in and of itself, an interesting experience, and one that helps you to become more mindful of your environment when you are not meditating.

Walk With Nothing

Leave everything at home except minimal clothing (a shirt and pants or a dress; no underwear, coats, or shoes & socks) and the key to your front door.

Step out your front door.

If you are still inside, walk until you are outside your building. What is it like to walk through your building with no shoes?

Take a step outside.

Are you standing on the sidewalk? Grass? A porch made of wood or concrete? Something else?

What does the material feel like under your bare feet?

Take a deep breath in. What does the air smell like?

What sounds do you hear outside today?

What does it feel like to begin your walk with no money and no shoes on?

Begin your walk.

Pay attention to the world around you, and to your experience of it. How is today different than how you normally experience the world outside your front door?

Stay out as long as you like, taking a leisurely stroll around your neighborhood.

Pay attention to the world around you.

What is it like?

How is this different than usual?

When you finally get home, take out your meditation journal and write about your experience.

Walk With Nothing In The Ocean *(special environment)*

Grandmother Ocean is an ecosystem unto herself, one which we as a species once rose up from, and one which we as a society still need for an abundance of resources. She is also an ecosystem that we cannot breathe in. For all these reasons and more, she should be treated with a special degree of care and respect.

That said, there is nothing quite like a weightless Walk With Nothing in the ocean. It's an indescribable experience.

As with any other Walk With Nothing, lock everything you have with you in your car, excepting the car key and either a shirt and shorts, a loose one-piece dress, or a bathing suit.

If you're comfortable with it, the loose dress is recommended because it gives you a more intimate tactile experience with the water. But some men aren't comfortable in loose dresses.

As you walk towards the water, what does the sand feel like beneath your feet? Is it hot? Are there sharp pebbles or broken shells? Is it as soft and fine as flour?

What does the sunlight feel like against your skin? Is it hot out?

What kind of sounds are at this beach right now?

Are there seagulls here?

Can you hear human voices? If so, are they quiet or soft? Do you understand the language that is being spoken?

As you enter the water, what is the temperature like?

What does this temperature of water feel like against your skin?

Are there any fish or seaweed near where you entered the water?

Is anything other than the water touching your skin? What does it feel like?

What does it feel like to be weightless?

What does the water feel like against your skin now?

Stay in the water for as long as you like, enjoying the experience and paying attention to the details. Let your mind and body float in the water.

When you leave the water to return to your beach blanket or car, take out your meditation journal and write down what your experience was like.

Chapter 5: Healing White Light Fills You

This is an excellent meditation for beginners because it is relatively easy for most people to "hold the picture in your mind" or "visualize" white light. It gets the practitioner used to the experience of holding a mental image while following a set of verbal or written instructions at the same time.

This is a very simple visualization technique when compared to some of the more advanced meditations that you will find later in this book. However, many people find it hard to succeed at visualization-style meditation at all because visualization in general trips them up.

Either they find it difficult to multitask – breathing correctly, keeping the body relaxed, keeping the mind clear of everything except the guide's words, and holding the mental picture that the guide tells them to hold or move through – in the way that meditation requires, or they don't realize all the diverse components of successful meditation even exist because no one ever explained to them what "pay attention to your breathing" means (please see the introductory chapter on breathing for a full explanation).

As always, the important thing to remember is to breathe in through the nose & out through the mouth as discussed in Chapter One, and to continue to focus on your breathing while following the instructions that you hear or read.

The next most important thing to do is to hold the image until your guide tells you to remove it, and to follow directions precisely. This may seem obvious or easy to do, but many people find it difficult at first because of the reasons listed above.

Another obstacle to following a guided meditation is that the idea of following a guide is distasteful to many people in our hyper-autonomous culture. To "let someone into your head" and obey their commands is a sign of weakness in so many situation, why would following a guide be any different? Why court the experience at all?

The reasons people pursue meditation are similar to the reason that people "veg out" to TV (which is a state of trance, incidentally) which is that we need time to be physically awake but not mentally active in order to keep our sanity. While in this "veg out" state of mind, we are susceptible to the images and concepts that are introduced to us through pictures, words, sounds, or other sources. The ingestion of these concepts is called hypnosis.

Unfortunately, the advertisers and programmers on TV aren't usually worried about their hypnotized viewers' well-being, they are often trying to sell products. With guided meditation, on the other hand, a responsible guide does have the well-being of the client in mind. We are not used to believing that strangers care what happens to us, however, which is the final nail in the coffin on the issue.

When looked at this way, we can see why so many people are afraid of meditation, and deride it as useless or scoff at its benefits. The great irony is that it is hypnosis via repetition – merchandise, movies, TV, etc– that has instilled in us this value of unyielding "independence" in the first place!

True independence, incidentally, is not isolation from others and an "I can do it myself!" attitude when "it" is inducing an excess of stress and is not logically something the individual can handle alone – that type of isolation is called immaturity. Real independence, on the other hand, comes from autonomous action and thought that contributes something to one's own existence and the environment in which one lives.

With autonomy, both real and culturally instilled, being valued as highly as it is, our own inner minds are the most sacred of unspoiled, private space. Or so we think. However, because we have already been (and continue to be) hypnotized by the created world around us – and other people can be part of the hypnotic effect since they have been hypnotized themselves, living in the same culture – we are now struggling to un-hypnotize ourselves by ourselves, and the *idea* of someone else undoing all the work we've done, or re-hypnotizing us via guided meditation is scary.

The thing is, guided meditation isn't re-hypnosis and there is nothing weak about participating in it. It is a type of holistic relaxation therapy that requires trust of the guide and of yourself, a commitment to the hard work and continuous practice that successful meditation requires, and dedication to their own improved well-being on the part of the practitioner: in short, hard work..

In most things, "working harder" means keeping the mind active, muscle tension, possible physical pain due to physical effort, and an addition of stress to the mind. The major difference here is that in mediation "working harder" means allowing yourself to relax and let go of tension and stress, while still allowing your waking mind to function passively (trance state). It takes some getting used to, but the health benefits and greater internal sense of well-being is worth the effort.

Whether it's an issue of psychosomatic recovery or an actual energy healing that takes place, Healing White Light meditations are shown to be present in treatment regimes that work. Also, when the meditations are continued as part of ongoing treatment for after care patients, quality of life and longevity have been shown to be higher than regimens that do not include meditation and mindfulness exercises.

One of the big things we are going to learn with this meditation is how to hit "trance state" intentionally, while in a place (the guided meditation) where we know the suggestions implanted are to our benefit.

Trance state is when your mind is functioning and awake, but passive.

Normally our minds are active as long as we are awake, except when "vegging out" or "spacing out." The former has been discussed; the latter, though it feels floaty and relaxed, is actually a hyper-focus not unlike more advanced guided meditations but not induced consciously and done without a guide.

While our minds are active the "noise" of the outside world is constantly seeping into our brains, and we are constantly reacting to it, each in our different ways.

An example of this is the type of music we normally hear when we visit the waiting room at a doctor's office. Some of us hear that music and it clicks the button in our brains that says "well, nothing to do now but sit back and wait" and we sit back in a chair, perhaps pick up a magazine, and *relax* and wait.

Others of us hear the music and associate it with childhood sickness and possibly scary visits to doctors' offices where we were poked and prodded while we already weren't feeling very well.

For those of us with this reaction to the music, the wait will be a very different, very tense experience. This tension can manifest physically as rigidity, nervous twitches, or babbling.

There are, of course, other possible manifestations of discomfort and reactions to waiting-room music, but this example illustrates how one button pushed by outside noise can effect people very differently.

Think of different sounds in your life, and how you react to them: the TV on, a radio playing, a friend talking while you're reading a magazine, and so on; add your own items.

Now think of someone you're close to, and about how they react to the sound stimuli on your list. Not quite exactly the way you do, is it?

That's because noise is incorporated differently by different people, depending how it effected them in the past. Generally, repeated stimuli or stimuli directly inserted to deeper levels of consciousness will stick more strongly than will more limited or superficial stimuli.

Trance state happens naturally and is a deeper level of consciousness.

Remember the child sick at the doctor's office? Chances are his or her mindset was in trance at the time; children hit natural trance very often because they have very little to stop them from doing so, and trance is the mind's natural resting state between sleep and being fully alert and active.

Think about it logically using the example of a child and her mother going to the grocery store.

The mother must worry about keeping the child in sight and safe, driving the car, getting the items on the list, finding these items, finding the shortest check-out line, stopping the child from putting candy into the cart, and so on. Her mind is fully active and alert because it has to be in order for her to successfully accomplish her tasks.

Her daughter, on the other hand, has no such need for mental focus. She happily rides in the basket or, if old enough, walks next to the cart, babbling on about cartoons or whatever else is in her mind, changing topics often as thoughts flit through her head, reaching out to the shelves for anything that looks shiny, pretty, or yummy.

Sounds a little bit like how you felt on your Walk With Nothing, doesn't it? That child is in a trance state, feeling nothing but joy, trust that her Mother will protect her and take care of everything (which she will) and curiosity about the world around her.

Ladies and gentlemen, meditation is about becoming more childlike. That is step one.

To achieve that end, the two trance-oriented self-propelled Beginner meditations in this book (Walk With Nothing and Healing White Light Fills You) should be practiced in some sort of rotation, meditating once daily, until a trance state can be consciously reached and maintained.

Healing White Light Fills You:

*Turn on some soft, soothing music that has **no** words or "wake up!" energy to it*

Sit in a chair that is comfortable and supports your body properly, or lie down.

Close your eyes.

Take a deep breath in through your nose,

hold it,

and let it out through your mouth.

Again; in through the nose, out through the mouth.

Review the introductory chapter on diaphragmatic breathing if you are having problems relaxing through breath alone.

If you are still having problems relaxing after that, go back and do a Tense and Release Meditation.

Once you are relaxed, keep breathing and begin to visualize:

As I count backwards from 10 to one, I want you to imagine a bright, almost blindingly beautiful white light.

There is nothing else, just the light.

Let it fill your vision completely as the numbers drop.

10 - remember to breathe in through the nose, hold, out through the mouth

9

8

7 - the light is beautiful

6

5

4 - let the radiance fill you

3

2

1

There it is, hovering above your head. Take a moment to bask in its radiance.

Pause

Now, imagine your own body.

 Anywhere you feel pain, tension, or stress, I want you to imagine it as a dark purple cloud.

Pause

Let the brilliant white light flow into you.

Everywhere that it contacts a purple cloud,

let the light fill the space and dissipate the cloud,

filling that part of your body with healing radiance.

Pause

Let the light continue to flow into your body, dissipating clouds.

Pause

Let the light continue to flow into your body, dissipating clouds.

Pause

Let the light continue to flow into your body, dissipating clouds.

Pause

Let the light continue to flow into your body, dissipating clouds.

Pause

You are now completely illuminated in brilliant white light, and the last of the purple clouds have dissipated.

Feel how good it is to be healthy, energized, and calm.

Long pause

Feel this light illuminate your entire body.

As I count upwards from 1 to 10, allow the light to remain,

invigorating you,

leaving you feeling healthy,

refreshed,

and relaxed

even after the meditation.

1

2

3

4

5

6

7

8

9

10

Open your eyes,

blink,

wiggle your toes,

shake out your arms and legs,

and stretch.

Welcome back. How do you feel?

Chapter 6: Mindful Motion Meditation

As we continue to get more advanced in our meditation practice, we start incorporating various elements in addition to visualizing and breathing.

Much like in a Walk With Nothing meditation, Mindful Motion meditations utilize the body. However, unlike a Walk With Nothing, Mindful Motion's focus is not the 5 senses, but rather the internal mind and *chi* or energetic life-force.

Lift up your hand. How did you do that? What does it feel like to do that? Lift your leg. How did you do that? How does anybody do anything? What is the mover behind the motion? Do our bones move our muscles? Do our muscles move our bones? Where are we lifting from, and who are "we" who is lifting at all? The answer is *chi*.

The point of a Mindful Motion meditation is to become more aware of our *chi*. I mentioned *Tai chi* in an earlier chapter; we have reached the point in our journey where we will be experiencing this type of meditation. Mindful Motion meditations are not unlike *Tai' Chi*, with the main difference being that *Tai' Chi* has the spiritual goal of consciously manipulating the *chi* life force that flows through the body as its goal.

If practiced daily, Mindful Motion meditations will also bring you to the point where you are moving your *chi* consciously through your body to precisely control your movements, strengthen your limbs, and increase blood circulation. However, unlike *Tai' Chi*, this is not the goal of a Mindful Motion meditation, so the way the mind is focused is slightly different. The goal of a Mindful Motion meditation is as the name implies: to become more mindful of our motions and our bodies so we are able to move around safely while in a state of trance This will become invaluable later when we learn to do As Spirit Moves You dancing meditations.

Mindful Motion Meditation:

Begin by standing with your feet your shoulders' width apart (male) or your hips' width apart (female) or slightly wider.

Bend both knees, and rest your weight evenly on both feet.

Feel how each foot and leg feels as it holds exactly half your body weight.

Place your hands in front of you in a classic prayer pose, palms flat together, elbows out to the sides & not touching your torso.

Take a deep breath in through your nose.

Release it, exhaling out all the tension from your body and relaxing more fully into the pose.

Do this again.

Keep breathing, in and out, feeling your spine relax into alignment.

If your posture doesn't correct itself automatically, place your feet together and straighten your legs.

Touch your toes.

Then, start at the base of your spine, and align the bottom vertebrae with your tail bone.

Do this instead of standing up "normally" (the "normal" way to stand is by lifting yourself internally from the shoulders until standing).

Stack the next vertebrae on top of the bottom one, and the next, and so on.

As you stack your vertebrae, allow your arms to hang limp in front of you.

Resist the urge to lift from the shoulders – they should be the last body part to rise, before the vertebrae of the neck, also one by one, and finally the head.

Now that you are standing up straight, legs apart, knees bent, chin slightly elevated, shoulders relaxed back, weight evenly distributed, you are ready to begin the meditation.

Pay attention to your breathing: in through the nose, out through the mouth.

Inhale, hold, exhale, hold, and inhale.

Feel your diaphragm inflate and your shoulders stay relaxed and back.

Continue breathing.

After you have read this section, put the book down and close your eyes.

Continue breathing.

Do not pick up this book again until you are fully in trance state, as described in the Healing Light Meditation chapter.

We are going to go through the motions of jumping jacks while in trance state.

The pose you are already in with be the first pose, called "ready stance."

From here, slowly let your body flow into second pose, "down,"

by lowering your hands while keeping them together until your fingertips are pointing straight down, while shifting your weight deeper into the floor by bending your knees further.

Be sure to keep your spine erect but not rigid while changing poses.

Next, flow into third pose, "up,"

by separating your hands in a natural circular motion and bringing them away from each other and up around the sides of your body to meet again above your head, *as you would if you were doing a jumping jack.*

As you are doing this, begin straightening your legs without moving your feet, and shifting your body weight upwards as you raise your arms.

Stretch your body up and reach for the ceiling with your fingertips.

Once you are in "up," repeat the cycle back to "ready stance" pose

by slowly dropping your weight back down,

letting your knees bend as they catch and hold your body weight.

As you do this, lower your hands, still in prayer position, back down to mid-chest and hold them there.

Continue breathing.

Repeat this cycle several times until you are satisfied with your practice for the day, or until your trance breaks naturally.

Do not be alarmed if your trance breaks naturally and often the first several times you perform this meditation, just continue on to the next posture.

Patience and practice will win out, and you will successfully incorporate the body into your meditation practice while in trance.

Chapter 7: Rainbow Chakra Meditation

In learning our Healing White Light meditation, we learned to visualize. We are now going to take the visualization a step further and hold several images at once, while still concentrating on our breathing and maintaining a trance.

You can absolutely succeed at doing this if you have followed the instructions in the Beginners chapters and did your daily practice. At this point, the Healing White Light meditation should be something that you can do without the book, and I recommend that if you find yourself in a stressful situation at work, on a bus or commuter train, dealing with family issues, or any other high stress event where you can excuse yourself to a rest room or at least close your eyes to visualize and breathe, that you should do so.

I find "quickie" meditations help quite a bit in the moment when stress is being caused if I am able to get one in. If you are not at the point in your practice with the Healing White Light meditation where you are nodding your head as you read this paragraph, my suggestion is to continue your daily practice with the beginner meditations until you are, then come back here and read on.

Rainbow Chakra Meditation:

Before doing this meditation, read through it and be sure that you understand all the instructions

Lie on the floor on your back.

Throughout this meditation, remember to breathe in through your nose and out through your mouth.

Close your eyes.

Take a deep breath in through your nose, hold it, and let it out through your mouth.

Again; in through the nose, out through the mouth.

Once you are relaxed, keep breathing and being to visualize:

As I count backwards from 10 to one, I want you to imagine a bright, almost blindingly beautiful white light.

There is nothing else, just the light.

Let it fill your vision completely as the numbers drop.

10 - remember to breathe in through the nose, hold, out through the mouth

9

8

7 - the light is beautiful

6

5

4 - let the radiance fill you

3

2

1

Bask in this radiance.

Pause

See your body as it is on the floor.

Imagine a swirling ball of pure, radiant red light at the base of your spine.

Hold the image.

Feel your solid connection to the earth anchor and comfort you.

As you watch the ball of red light swirl in a clockwise motion, feel it's glow warm your body, starting at the tailbone and spreading out as the ball expands.

Watch the ball get bigger and bigger until it completely engulfs your pelvis.

As it continues to swirl clockwise, shift your focus upwards slightly, to just below your belly button.

Imagine a swirling ball of pure, radiant orange light just below your belly button.

Hold the image.

Feel your creativity flourish and expand.

As you watch the ball of orange light swirl in a clockwise motion, feel it's glow warm your body, starting just below your belly button and spreading out as the ball expands.

Watch the ball get bigger and bigger until it completely engulfs your lower back and stomach.

As it continues to swirl clockwise, shift your focus upwards slightly, to just above your belly button.

Imagine a swirling ball of pure, radiant yellow light just above your belly button.

Hold the image.

Feel your gut instincts, in tune with reality, lead you true.

As you watch the ball of yellow light swirl in a clockwise motion, feel it's glow warm your body, starting just below your belly button and spreading out as the ball expands.

Watch the ball get bigger and bigger until it completely engulfs your mid back and upper abdominal region.

As it continues to swirl clockwise, shift your focus upwards slightly, to your heart.

Imagine a swirling ball of pure, radiant green light engulf your heart.

Hold the image.

Feel the sensation of love within your heart.

As you watch the ball of green light swirl in a clockwise motion, feel it's glow warm your body, starting at your heart and spreading out as the ball expands.

Watch the ball get bigger and bigger until it completely engulfs your chest and upper back.

As it continues to swirl clockwise, shift your focus upwards slightly, to your throat.

Imagine a swirling ball of pure, radiant blue light engulf your throat.

Feel your ability to speak and communicate flourish.

Hold the image.

As you watch the ball of blue light swirl in a clockwise motion, feel it's glow warm your body, starting at your heart and spreading out as the ball expands.

Watch the ball get bigger and bigger until it completely engulfs your neck and shoulders all the way up to your mouth

As it continues to swirl clockwise, shift your focus upwards slightly, to the spot between your eyes called the Third Eye.

Imagine a swirling ball of pure, radiant indigo light engulf your Third Eye.

Hold the image.

Feel your awareness flourish and your intelligence and thoughts flow like water.

As you watch the ball of indigo light swirl in a clockwise motion, feel it's glow warm your body, starting at your heart and spreading out as the ball expands.

Watch the ball get bigger and bigger until it completely engulfs your head.

As it continues to swirl clockwise, shift your focus upwards slightly, to the spot at the very top of your head.

Imagine a swirling ball of pure, radiant violet light engulf the top of your head.

Hold the image.

Feel your connection to deity and the universe expand and flourish.

As you watch the ball of violet light swirl in a clockwise motion, feel it's glow warm your body, starting at the top of your head and spreading out as the ball expands.

Watch the ball get bigger and bigger until it completely engulfs your head.

As it continues to swirl clockwise, return your focus to your entire body.

You are radiant with swirling light in all the colors of the rainbow, and you feel wonderful – completely relaxed, healthy, and balanced.

Feel this light illuminate your entire body.

As I count upwards from 1 to 10, allow the light to remain, invigorating you, leaving you feeling healthy, refreshed, and relaxed even after the meditation.

1

2

3

4

5

6

7

8

9

10

Open your eyes, blink, wiggle your toes,
shake out your arms and legs, and stretch.

Welcome back. How do you feel?

Chapter 8: Focus Meditation

Now that we have learned to let our thoughts go and reach a trance consciously, the next step is to learn how to focus on an object, topic or concept while meditating. The object focused on is called a *mantra*, and can be a picture, a sound such as the stereotypical "om," a phrase one repeats over and over to one's self, or some other form.

The idea of a mantra is twofold: one, mantras help many individuals to gain a trance state more quickly; two, mantras make it possible to use a trance to gain insight. An example we are all familiar with is a Buddhist monk repeating the "om" sound in order to gain spiritual insight. Interestingly enough, the "om" sound is actually the first sound of a word in a phrase, with the phrase being the mantra and the monk taking it piece by piece to be thorough. The monk is feeling the first sound of the phrase through his entire body, resonating with it until there is no choice but to open his mouth and release it to the universe.

While this is happening, the monk is aware of the surface meaning of the entire phrase. If he has been meditating for a long time, he probably also has deeper insights into the words he is using as a mantra, as well as that meaning's integration into the whole of existence.

That continued ability to gain new insights, in this case insights of a spiritual nature regarding a phrase and using the phrase as a catalyst for deeper insights, is the whole point of mantra meditation.

Many people teach mantra meditation as the most basic of beginner's meditations. I admit this is useful if working with a client who needs to tackle a specific issue in his or her life through meditation, such as coping with a recent event that negatively effected him or her, but for the serious student of meditation, this is not a helpful thing to do.

This is because although mantras are very useful if someone wants to meditate "on" something in order to reach a conclusion about it, if people try to learn how to hit trance in the first place through a mantra, then they never learn how to let go completely and allow the passive mind state which is so vital to meditation to occur fully.

This chapter will contain two mantra meditations, a visual one and an oral one. This is because different types of mantras will work better for different people, depending on the individual.

Visual Mantra Meditation:

Please look around you and pick something to focus on. If nothing seems especially attention-getting, feel free to focus on the picture of the dolphins on the front of this book.

Let your mind wander a you gaze at your mantra.

Wonder about it.

Daydream about it.

Look at it.

As you continue to let your thoughts flow over each other about this thing you are focusing on, remember to

breathe in deeply through your nose,

hold the air in your lungs,

exhale out through your mouth,

hold the out-breath,

and breathe in deeply through your nose again

in a continuous cycle.

Continue to let your thoughts flow as you stare at your mantra. **At the end of this paragraph put down this book and focus completely on your breathing and your object.** When you feel satisfied that you have pondered this object while in trance to your satisfaction, pick the book back up and begin reading again where it says "resume reading here."

Oral Mantra Meditation:

Please carefully read the phrase "I like music."

Let your mind realize the obvious meaning first, then think about what the phrase "I like music" means to you.

Repeat it out loud to yourself: say "I like music." How did that change the flow of your thoughts?

Repeat it again,

now again,

now again.

Say the word "I."

Who are you?

Say "I like."

What does that mean?

Now say "I like music."

What does that mean right now?

Do you like the sound of music?

Do you enjoy dancing to it?

Can you feel music in your body when you hear it?

Did a certain type of music start playing in your head?

Ponder these questions lazily.

Allow yourself to daydream about the phrase "I like music."

If you feel the desire to at any point, repeat the phrase out loud again, or part of it, as many times as you wish.

Perhaps you noticed that repeating the first sound in "like" sounds like a song: li-li-li-li-li, or that repeating the first sound in "music" sounds like a singing cow: mu-mu-mu.

Continue to let your thoughts drift and put the book down when you are done reading this section:

Put on some music, preferably without words, and hold in your mind the sentence "I like music."

React with movement, stillness, singing, silence – in short, react however you wish, so long as you don't lose your trance.

To get to trance, focus on the sentence "I like music"

while breathing in through your nose,

holding it,

out through your mouth,

hold,

and back in again through your nose.

Pick up the book and continue reading where it says "resume reading here" on the next page when you feel satisfied that your meditation is over.

Resume reading here Now that you have done a mantra meditation, you may be having one of several different types of reactions.

You may have gotten nothing out of it.

You may have gotten very much out of it, in which place it is time to start an entry in your meditation journal.

Grab a notebook or flip to the blank pages at the end of this book, write down any insights that you have experienced this session (and anything else that you feel is significant) along with today's date and what number session this is – i.e., how many mantra meditations have you done before this one? Also record that this was a mantra meditation and the time of day when it took place.

Keeping a journal is invaluable for marking progress in your meditative journey and for remembering insights later, after they have been dulled by time, while they are still fresh and vivid.

All mantra meditations should be attempted once a day for a week before giving up on them if you do not experience anything right away.

If you feel that you chose the wrong type of focus for your mantra, feel free to switch objects or even to the other sensory type listed, but, if you switch, begin the 7 days of the mantra meditation fresh with the new focus.

Chapter 9: Disciplined Moving Meditation

Disciplined Moving Meditation will take the skills we learned in Mindful Motion Meditation and add an extra variable: music. Music is an outside stimulus, so the goal is to incorporate an outside stimulus, including our body-moving reaction to it, smoothly into our internal-focus body-motion meditation.

Sound impossible? It's not. It is, however, rather difficult, and will take quite a bit of practice and patience to accomplish. I have faith in you, my reader: anyone who has gotten as far as you have in a book like this already possesses those vital traits.

In *Tai' Chi*, the mind is consciously focused on not thinking or controlling the body's movements, so the *chi* can control the body's motion without the mind getting in the way. In Mindful Motion meditation, the opposite is the case: the practitioner focuses only on the body and its movements while the meditation is taking place. The body and its motions, in essence, becomes the meditation practitioner's mantra. In a Disciplined Moving Meditation (DMM), the mantra is the interaction between the body's movements and the music being heard.

Disciplined Movement Meditations are not As The Spirit Moves You meditations. They are called "disciplined motion" for a reason: each action is prepared ahead of time, and then repeated in a precise order when the meditation occurs. This allows the meditation practitioner to gain and hold trance while maintaining movement, thanks to our (now) familiar friend: repetition.

In this case, repetition is about repetition of motion to the same song, rather like practicing a dance routine for an audience.

The difference between DMM and performance, however, is that in DMM the practitioner is focused on how it feels to perform each motion in time to the music, rather than how it will look on stage when this is done.

Anyone reading this who is a practitioner of the performing arts already knows most of what I'm talking about: the ability to do this, or hit *fugue,* is what separates the truly fantastic performer from the garden-variety actor or dancer.

The *fugue* state, or melding of an artist's self with the medium he or she is using, which in this case is body language and timing, is the goal of a Disciplined Moving meditation.

In order to do this properly, we must use motions which everyone is familiar with.

When I lead a group doing DMM, I am able to demonstrate what I do first, then everyone follows and repeats my motions, rather like when people take an aerobics class, although with DMM the motions are slower and more deliberate, and everyone is in or attempting to be in a trance state. People who practice aerobics at home with the same video everyday may well have reached a *fugue* for the span of time when that is happening.

Because I am unable to demonstrate motions, we are going to use the ones from

"I'm a Little Teapot." You may think that this is silly; you're right, it is. Go ahead and laugh now; get it out of your system.

When you are ready to take the meditation seriously, continue reading.

If at any point during the meditation you find yourself feeling embarrassed or silly, just remember: childlike openness is a goal.

If you can draw on childhood memories of performing "I'm a Little Teapot" and having fun while doing it, and then repeat that enjoyment as an adult, you're already halfway to *fugue*.

The next element is music. Because we all know the song, sing right now "I'm a little teapot."

Now, go to your music library and select an instrumental song that is slower than the pace you are used to singing this song at; remember, the movements will be slower and more deliberate, as in a Mindful Motion meditation.

Once you have selected the song, play it and sing along to it using the lyrics from "I'm a little teapot."

Sing this song over and over again while the music plays through until the song ends. Listen to this song often, and continuously sing along.

When you are at the point where when you hear the song you automatically sing the "teapot" lyrics in your head, you are ready to incorporate body motions and move on to the actual meditation, as described below:

Read through this meditation before performing it.

Perform the body motions at least once after reading it through before adding the music.

It is wise to perform the poses several times before adding music, until they are natural and comfortable, as learned in the section on Mindful Motion meditations.

Disciplined Moving Meditation

Take a deep breath in through your nose.

Release it, exhaling out all the tension from your body and relaxing more fully into the pose.

Do this again.

Keep breathing, in and out, feeling your spine relax into alignment.

Now that you are standing up straight, legs apart, knees bent, chin slightly elevated, shoulders relaxed back, weight evenly distributed, you are ready to begin the meditation.

Keep paying attention to your breathing: in through the nose, out through the mouth.

Inhale, hold, exhale, hold, and inhale.

Feel your diaphragm inflate and your shoulders stay relaxed and back.

Continue breathing.

Take the first teapot pose: "teapot."

Placing your hands on your hips, elbows out, while maintaining your erect posture.

Sing the line with the music.

Take the second pose: "handle."

Lift one arm up from your waist to eye level and turn your fingers away from you.

Be sure all five fingertips are touching each other.

Sing the line with the music.

Keep breathing in thorough your nose, hold, out through your mouth, hold, and in through your nose.

Take the third pose: "steamed."

Lift your weight onto your tiptoes,

straighten your legs,

raise your chin and hand slightly,

and straighten out your raised arm so it is facing diagonally up and away from you.

Sing the line with the music.

Take the fourth and final pose: "pour."

Bending the knee beneath your upraised hand and shifting your body weight to that foot,

bend sideways at the waist,

lean forward,

and angle your body downwards in a slow, controlled motion

while slowly lowering your upraised hand until it is touching the floor near your foot *(if you are not flexible enough to touch the floor, go as low as you comfortably can).*

Sing the line.

The final motion is the cycle back from "pour" to "teapot."

Shifting your weight back to your straightened leg,

bend it at the knee until your body weight is again evenly distributed 50/50 on both legs.

As you are doing this, raise yourself off the floor so that your torso is sitting directly center between both legs,

and lift your arm so that your hand is again on your hip.

Remember to breathe in through the nose, hold, out through the mouth, hold, and back in through the nose.

Also be sure to maintain an erect but flexible spinal posture throughout the duration of the pose-shifting meditation in order to avoid cramps and injuries.

Repeat the action of flowing through the poses until the song ends.

When you have done this a few times, you may wish to play the song on repeat so that you can perform the cycle of repeating postures for as long as you wish while you are learning to induce fugue, and while you are in fugue.

The Tale of Wormy

Endnote

There once was a worm, and he was a happy little worm. He lived in a graveyard and had plenty of nutritious, rotting flesh in the dirt he ate, and so he grew up to be a big, strong worm, full of zest and life, y'know, for a worm. I would say that he was greatly admired by all the other worms, but they couldn't see him, nor he see them, because earthworms are blind.

One day, a huge rain came, and the graveyard's dirt flooded, as dirt does, causing all the worms to rise up and all the pigeons and seagulls from the area to search for a worm feast.

Now Wormy, our giant, healthy worm, was so big that he looked like two or three other worms, and so two or three birds picked up different parts of him and attempted to swallow him down whole. Imagine their surprise when Wormy was attached to two other birds!

Well, they struggled, and gulped, and poor Wormy was torn to pieces by this exchange, but the birds, who had never met each other before, became friends after that and always told other birds about the giant worm ("it was this big!") that it took all three of them to land. In the struggle, many other smaller worms got away.

Moral of the story?

You tell me

__Meditation Journal__

Be sure to include:

Date

Type of Meditation

Personal observations

Questions for next time

Meditation Journal

Meditation Journal

Meditation Journal

Meditation Journal

Meditation Journal

Meditation Journal

Meditation Journal

Meditation Journal

Meditation Journal

Meditation Journal

Meditation Journal

Meditation Journal

Meditation Journal

Meditation Journal

Meditation Journal

Meditation Journal

Meditation Journal

Meditation Journal

Meditation Journal

Meditation Journal

Meditation Journal

Meditation Journal

Meditation Journal

Meditation Journal

Meditation Journal

Meditation Journal

Meditation Journal

Meditation Journal

Meditation Journal

Meditation Journal

Meditation Journal

Meditation Journal

Meditation Journal

Meditation Journal

Meditation Journal

Meditation Journal

Meditation Journal

Meditation Journal

Meditation Journal

Meditation Journal

Meditation Journal

Meditation Journal

Meditation Journal

Meditation Journal

Meditation Journal

Meditation Journal

Meditation Journal

Meditation Journal

Meditation Journal

Meditation Journal

Meditation Journal

Meditation Journal

Meditation Journal

Meditation Journal

Meditation Journal

Meditation Journal

Meditation Journal

Made in the USA
Charleston, SC
23 December 2012